Break
through

Break
through

ROOPA R

PARTRIDGE
A Penguin Random House Company

To order additional copies of this book, contact
Partridge India
000 800 10062 62
orders.india@partridgepublishing.com

www.partridgepublishing.com/india

Contents

About the Book

Written intricately, Roopa R has assayed a wide range of heartfelt experiences and emotions in this collection. The collection varies from simple everyday situations to being deeply spiritual, thus catering to a wide variety of readers. Pick it up and you'll ask for more.

Acknowledgement

Editing credit : Ria V Matmari

Time waits for all ...
and suddenly for none.

Dedicated
To my dearest three...

Gift of sight

Valiant was your fight
In peaceful sleep you left aside
Your mortal remains of sight

Earthly boundaries you transcended
To enter heavenly doors
Leaving behind mortal eyes
To travel borders asight

To them your sight
To us your inner might
All your gestures big or small
Treasures in them all.

Healing tears

Baffled I was, with dropping jaw
When time stood still and tears froze,
With borrowed courage, I did emote
To an angel here and an angel there

My best day began when I heard you say
With a smile
There's nothing right, there's nothing wrong
For, my healing began.

Journey of self discovery

When you meet me
Think of me as divine
Drink from me less
Or drink from me more
For my spirit
Is all infinite

Gently leave imprints
Like sand dunes from gale tides
That sculpted beauty
Etch forlorn memories
Lingering beyond all times

So that memory reminisced
Between your absence
Takes me through life's jumbles
Till time arranges
Our meet again

If we sail through an island
Through good times and bad
Unwinding here and there

Like a cola's fizz
Unmasking till zeroes
Each in our own way
Just together

We might
Begin to understand ourselves
A whole lot better.

(1st Stanza : Divine implies asking to be identified at soul level
(in contrary to physical)
2nd Stanza : Imprint implies the protagonist asking the visitor
to leave lasting sensory memory to carry through till the
next meeting
4th Stanza : Unmasking till zeroes implies 'opening up'
5th Stanza : 'Each in our own way implies not impinging
on another's journey of self discovery)

Acceptance of death

Time the giver
Time the taker
As well as the receiver
Of life

The days you breathed faster
Life drained your eyes
I parched, voiceless
Swallowing salty tears

Your body spoke tiredness
While your wise mind listened
In life, you accepted death
Now in your death you've graced life.

Life complete

I want to tell you this
I want success
But measure me not with what I earn
I want power
To feel good, for a while
I want to live life completely
For life complete
Is all of good, bad and ugly.

Roopa R

My exams

My heart goes lub, my heart goes dub
End of the trail after sleepless nights
Did I step right?

A heartburn and a churn
Faces familiar seem unfamiliar
To questions posed I half whisper

With results come I delight in jump
I thank God for the hundredth time
For my delight.

Acceptance

Now I wonder
You left me asunder
And passed away
Did you and God together think
My toil has made me strong to tread?

For a while now
I've been living in the present
With time running out
I catching up with time

All my learning of yester years
Breathed acceptance unto me
Pushing hopes and denial aside
Sighting your mortal remains.

Unraveling myself

I want to unravel
Journeying unto myself
Shedding self consciousness

I want to throw all pretence
To the winds
That I may just be me.

Dole me time

Death knocked my door
To pluck a dear
In denial I slammed the door

Death knocked again
And whispering said
"It's about time"
I pleaded
Death understood

Loose ends to tie
Loved ones to hug
Many things unsaid
Only time can till.

Walk with us

God, in your world
If I believe that everything is good
And has its place
Of what use are cycles of misery, birth and death
Or tsunamis, cyclones and volcanoes?

Are these to keep us in place?
Or is there a predictable pattern
Learning which we can protect our brethren
While we walk in your loving Grace.

The laden path

God, I want to exploit you
For thou art limitless
That, I see faith when the going is thin
For, I hear thy voice in my quietude

Nudging me to tread thy path
Cleared of snow and storm
My time has come to tell the world
It's not the storm I see around
For in stillness you guide my calm.

A crater in my chest

I have in me an effervescence
Spurred by man made woe
Laid in chest for eon years
Till hide in silence no more

Nature doled freely its abundance
From pasture filled berry and bough
Breathed beauty in my feelings
Etching a shimmery glow

Craters in chests
Are meant for frilled colors
That life may dance in snow.

RIP

It was less than a week ago
That I saw creases deep, on your face
Today you've left behind those creases
And walked to the land of peace

I wonder how many years of hammering it took
With grinding thoughts and feelings,
For longsome years

By as many men as women,
In sculpting your creases
Walking to the other side,
Now others will start their creases.

Stay with me

Dad I cried a hundred cries
But not one on your lap
I didn't know how
I cried for my failures
Hoping against hope

My tears are dry
I froze time
Whiling away years
As I step from boyhood to manhood
I want you to walk
Beside me.

Spiritual abundance

A decor of restraint clothed my shame
Which you named elegance
Much later
Wisdom taught me thus
Shame is nature's spiritual abundance
Read by Man otherwise.

God's time

What is your blueprint
For us and for you ?
On earth, at times slow is fast
What is your time line ?

The earthly time line for man
Shifts to your time line
In connection with you

Do you get enticed like us on earth
If so, who is your God ?
I know all these answers are in the Upanishads
Or wherever

Still manifest these to me and more
I'll make some time
Direct experience cannot replace reading.

Trust

When my eye fills my mind
With distrusting thoughts
Be it the smoke from a chimney or puff
May quickly my inner eye silence in faith
Guardian I'll be
But not always the best
Who can beat nature
In its masterly venture ?

Be Yourself

My heart cried a hundred cries
When you stopped laughing
When I saw your world fall apart
With peoples' eyes on you

Your feelings are real
Not meant to be slighted
Live, grow in your feelings
Till you are you

Life is not about modeling
In another's way
That way, you will never be you.

Dance life

Tell me again and again
With my brethren by my side
I'm not them and they are not me
That in loving life, I live my terms

That I forget not
To each his own
Life is not meant to be bartered
That way my life will never be mine

By this is meant thus
I can stand by you
While you take your decisions
All of them one by one.

Roopa R

Lord of time - Yama

Lord of time Yama, listen to my plea
Spare my friend and love,
From the transit of death
What's the hurry ?

In his recovery awaken him from slumber
In your wisdom grant him a boon
To guide others in their recovery
After all God needs Man to carry out his mission on earth
Use him, we sure will be with you.

Be Thyself

You are no boy or man
For God in His wisdom made you
And placed you before my eye

To let you flow like a river
And place no barricades
While you create your way

Knowing or unknowing
You teach me lessons
Of a lofty life

Have I no better business
Than place my eye
I'd rather let you grow
That you be all of you.

Change

I waited long enough
For the situation to change
And now finally
When the situation seems right
I realize
Only I have changed.

Pain.. bearing it all

I see pain in your eyes and look away
Long days and longer nights
You've borne it all the way

With mind in your reign access balms in your brain
Nature wants your wholeness not for no gain
Give what's your best and lay her to rest

Go into your mind, in closets you will find
Stacks of endorphins waiting to smile
One by one dancing to trickle
With strength of a hundred people

When you explore your pain
Ask its address again
For like you and me it may hide again
Saying what one likes but doing another

Having started, whatever else you let go,
Don't let this one go
Go to the root till you find fruit.
(Endorphins released from brain are known to
decrease pain and to be feel good factors)

Whither freedom?

Cloistered till I breathe no more
Pangs of fear chasing all doors
I scream so loud it deafens my ear
A slave laden in gold necklace
In balance I fear

Questions asked of me
In quick succession
Whither this ? Whither that ?
For some I have answers, for others none

Wielding my energy, in circles I run
Like a slave in a man's world
Waiting to lay golden eggs
But my boisterous energy killed one by one

I hide my pain in glamorous sham
Waiting for noises of dust to die
I'm tired, running for others lives
My wings all clipped to drain

Title of martyr or of crown
I lay them down
To chose freedom all my own
To write a script all too light

My eyes were blind to answers then
While I resisted things in vain
Life's rule of acceptance I learnt is key
That opens door to a many

Now I tread softly creating paths
To script history within or out
At times none but in comfort zone
Bartering resistance for acceptance

For now I've laid my questioning thoughts
That I lay in peace, just me with my thoughts.

(1st Stanza : expresses the protagonist's lack of
freedom in spite of material wealth
1st Stanza : 'In balance I fear' reveals that in spite of fear the
person is trying to go about keeping some kind of balance
3rd Stanza : indicates an energetic woman struggling hard
and patiently in search of an identity in a man's world
3rd Stanza : Golden eggs indicate creative expression
4th Stanza : 'Wings all clipped' indicate curtailing freedom
4th Stanza : 'To drain' means be drained of all energy)

Thank you cancer

Thirty years and a little more
Together we scored
Our ups and downs
Somehow pulling our feet

But t'was your cancer which taught me love
And brought back our romance
When you had no voice to speak
You lent my eyes your voice

You braved it all
Breathless walks, numbed feet
Sore gums and palate all gone
Yet, your verve for life, was not one cent down

With life complete
You'd said what you wanted
For time stood still
Has a better world beckoned you ?

Friends

As wind blows parting us fiercely
I'm parched for a vodka or two
Memories of booze and breeze

That was another life, another world
Shades of grey, with time slip by
At tether's end a reverse turn.

In silence we spoke

In silence I heard
Tuning my ear
With eyes that grazed thy mind

All time I read
With words a few
Till brimmed my heart anew

Contented minds
Contented souls
We had spoken all we had

Silence was no silence
For in it were answers
To questions asked and unasked

We were each other's
And time was all time
I got all answers
And you were no more

You were not you
Even before
You were more than you
You were, all in all, mine

In your sleeping too, you are mine
For your mortal remains
Is now in my immortal me.

A Soup to brew

Brew from your soup of yesteryears
With flavors every kind
That you pepper it now and then
On life's twists 'n turns

How many morrows did you wait ?
Before you pulled yourself
From the glue and rut of a downed life
Others can never know

Look down you did
Now just look up
There are ears a plenty
You'll feel a different kind

Come out of your sorrows
Clean board once more
Flavors are of different kind
Enjoy it all the more

Now and then
You may feel down again
Breathing deep, close your eyes
Sprinkle your peppers again

Let yesteryears go past by
Morrows have waited for long
Think not of steadiness
Nor of it all the while

Step into your today
Making it all alive
You will cover flavors
All in this one life.

The taste of life

Tell death to wait
It's not my turn now
For I listened when death told me to wait
And I wanted to die

For, I want to experience life
To tell the dry withering leaves
That they too look golden yellow

While driving back home,
I stop at the traffic junction
I want to stop and smile back at that auto* nearby

Don't stop me
While I appreciate the perfect teardrop
On that beggar's cheek

Can you wait ?
I want to tell you more.

(*Auto is a popular three wheeled cab in India)

Final release

My eyes are weary and closer home
In quiet peace and calm ease
I wait not for final release
In foggy minds brewing storm
In thickets filled with breeze

You promised me freedom, no doubt
But how will you relieve yourself from your shackles ?
For you yourself are stuck in one
Close your eyes
Count not the distance between us
We are one.

Daddy

You braided my hair
And cycled me home to school
You gave me wings a tad too early
Down into boarding school

Much later I learned
My unfinished school
In hidden memories
The chatter and patter

It took me time to forgive you
All distance stuffed in tears
My tears spoke faster than words
'Coz papa I loved you.

Holding on

It's less than two morrows
When sparrows chirped
And time stood still

Holding hands
Temples and tides
Mountains and valleys
We sighted

I overlooked the grey in my tresses
Whence time tried telling me
For long
All that it wanted to

With you, were things on a platter
Whence I nagged and pouted
Today I'm alone but wise

Have I loved you enough
To let you go
Ere the final good bye ?

Labor

All houses are the same
Only some home here and there
How can I question you not
In your work and play

Nature's pull is far too full
Swirling in a pool
Earthly time will suffice not
When you want to be upright

How many winters have passed by
How many summers are waiting more ?
Breathe your full, take your time
Tread step one by one

In all you do, think and do
In your silence winter will favor you
No work is small or big
Hasten to tell your mind

Think not of labor's fruit
That will come in time
Its nature's law
It needs no contest.

Revolt

I revolted standing in the rain
Doing forbidden things all in vain
Wanting acceptance
I pouted and experimented

I followed nature's ways
Doing what grownups did
With burning anger and seething fury
All care hanging in air

Every story is more than a story
Dented here and there
Coded genes holding secrets tight
Waiting till seen as sacred might

In mundane routine
I pray for health
In tempered tone I pray for wealth
Aging wisdom blinds me not

Cycle of nature manifests
Reminding history here and there
Closing my eyes I turn away
Before nature's fury turns awry.

My eyes on your soul

I delve into reality
With you in the foray
A trail is formed

Between falling crumbs
Closer to reality I'm brought
Chocochips, pudding and pie
Smiling eye to eye

A perfect beat of a heart's drum
Tongue tied my mind is stunned
Gazing all in balance

My cup is full
At my sight of you
Layer after layer, for the crumble of sham
I wait to fall

When all is done
Now there comes a smile
Wide on my face
For you've bared your soul

You are all of life
With time at hand
You chatter things, I want not to hear
Just your soul and mine, side by side
That, I meet my bliss inside

And then I listen
Your chatter makes sense
It's finding trust within
I say not yes, I say not no
I just say "is it ?"

I see you smile
You muster strength
To live your life.

Growing wings

If like a hawk
I rest my eyes on you
You will never grow

Build your nest
In time you'll learn to fly
And my eyes can rest in ease.

My diva

I watch
Your tresses peppered silvery grey
All gestures laced with grace
Could it be that you've been through
All that I've been and more ?

For you feel every feeling
Even before I feel
And know every thought much before I think

You welcome me with open arms
Pointing not this nor that
I know you must have accepted thyself
Far more than I've accepted me

For how else can you be all of these
And see a flawless me ?

(Both 'Healing tears' and 'My diva' are meant for people
in the healing profession which include counselors)

My Universe

I'm still figuring my place in this world
Am I a speck or the very Universe ?
(In the above line whereas 'speck' implies being a part of the whole
universe, in contrast, the phrase 'the very Universe' indicates an
individual being empowered by the universal power completely)

Finding myself

I branded myself a closed box
Until I found one like you
For you heard, when I chattered
To feel joy, to feel pain
That my numbness downs the drain.

(The above lines indicate that a numbed mind
can find an outlet by venting out in a proper setting)

Blurred tears

I can hear you want to say something
But I know not what
And know not how to ask

I can be beside you,
Till you've said all that you want
And hear what I want to say

Our tears may blur to heal
When walls break down
And only love remains

When you know not,
If there's enough time or not
We've got to pick that courage to trust
That we may open up.

My eyes watch you

You brave sorrows into nothingness
And walk with grace for miles
Is it your yesteryears of struggle,
That makes your living worthwhile ?
Did winters teach you resilience,
As summers lovely smiles ?

(The above was derived as an inspiration by watching
a woman deserted by her wayward spouse, gathering
herself courageously to lead a respectable life)

Dormant tunes

I want to relive the taste of butterscotch
Long after it has melted in my mouth
And the ruffles lays
Which I tasted yesterday

I want to listen to that song again
To catch up with what it had to say
And live that tune and that note
I want to live these things
For I have missed it yesterday.

Wild child

You are God's child
You wander in wilderness
Even before the wind beckons you
Tell me what's your thought
Tell me your impulse

When I can see you no further
Than a tiny dot
Teach me lessons
That make me strong

You've trespassed boundaries
Answering minds call
And abandoned treasures
Craving dicey paths

Show me birds fly from nests
Tell me you can fly
Show me what's
Written on your kite
That I gently let go by.

My web

I may enchant you with my dove like eye
With chirpy talk, till a soothing sigh
Pools of laughter rippling through
To die at break of dawn

Grounded root, brought more strength than can
Until I realized t'was meant not just for me
It took me time to mend my heart
Hardened life melted, till raw tears shed
Jilted by love, an illusion of rainbow

Repressed feelings wrung twisted thoughts
Searching for ebbs and tides
Seething anger in my mind
Why did I go wrong ?

When I'm done, a voice soothes me
To forgive myself and forgive my love
For, if I don't, was my motive right ?
That only I can answer.

Making of identity

I want to be there for me
To feel every feeling of mine
When I feel the pangs of jealousy,
Of anxiety
When I'm drowned in deep desperation
I want to stay there
And walk out of my feelings
While the fibre that's me
Maketh me.

Brahma

I've experienced you
And am still in awe

When my beloved transcended
Leaving his mortal remains
To unite unto you
Did your grace dissolve him
In the infinity of your unconditional love
That he became you?

My face alights
Reminiscing my experience of you
I proceed no further in what I'm doing

I'm dumb stuck, in awareness
You are all love, all acceptance
All knowing, you hear with not our ears
And see with sight not like ours

In proximity with love, not like the skin that clothes
You knew of things afar, even when not near
In death people unite and become you
Is my spouse of this life with you?

If I could experience you
Time and again while living
I realize
All else in life is for tilling
Reveling in you
Everything is awareness, awareness is You.

In you is everything, with nothing to add
You've graced me
And I'm Thy blessed earthly child

Shunya* on earth
Is the path to Unity♦ of afterlife
Remind me to walk with you
That I may revel in whatever I do

My mind tells me that with you in proximity
No wrong is wrong
All actions fall like scales of snake
For you are nonjudgmental
All the tilling is for my conscience, not you.

*Shunya (zero, nothingness) ♦Unity (completeness)

Hassle free

I imagine
If it were that I learn
To take my basket full of woes
And place them aside

I'd explore my very being
And get back
To where I was
My thoughts would be breezed.

Small truths and big

Mundane things
Are small truths made big
The real truth is only love
Love is all

Love to forgive, love to move on
Love to work and live
Why fret and fume for small things
Or is nothing too small ?

What things are big and what things small ?
It's in the thinking all
A tree from a seed
Says it all.

Life's mission

In the coziness of life
I've hardly worked
Or so I feel
Looks like keeping quiet at times
Is bigger work

Now I know not
What work is in store
Through me, will you walk with people ?
Listening to them
That's what I foresee for me

For, listening unburdens to empower
I've heard it often
'Carry not another's burden'
Including your brethrens
So God, while I listen, speak through me

Being everywhere
Empowers you to listen, to see
To walk with man through people
Enchanting them with you who are
Sweeter than the sweetest being.

Son

For all these years
You've remained my little one
I'm sorry, I haven't learnt to let go
I was lost in my world and couldn't hear you
While you screamed, your hundred screams

Forgive me in whole
That, before I pass, I rest in peace
Forgive me for being a passive observer
While you were being bantered

In my life's journey
I've tasted peace
Today you stand before me in whole
Until you unite with your beloved
Pardon me for my many shortcomings
All one by one

My wisdom taught me courage
To ask your forgiveness
Forgive me
You too will rest in ease.

Empowered calmness

I enticed you with my bubbly mirth
Till I touched your soul
Now you are far yet near
In your quietude you guide me

With you here I shirked no end
Acting a plain Jane
Now you are gone
Empowering me
For things undone

I want not to trouble you
After you reach heaven
And that's why
This hurried conversation

Sooner than later
You'll be calmness personification
Knowing my *Brahma
It could be even before the sooner

You had said all you wanted to
I too had said mine
I'm saying the little things unsaid
Before the final goodbye.

*Brahma is supreme consciousness
[Written during the fourteen days ceremony period after death. In the
Hindu philosophy it is believed that the soul reaches heaven on the 14th day]

Roopa R

Goddess of time

You portray a picture of illusion
When things happen un-understood
Infusing through things earthly
Like tumultuous tsunami tide

In thickets we stick
Till we leave behind the stink
To be pruned from silkworm to silk
For a tiny glimmer of hope

Standing in awe with clenched teeth
Knowing not what to do
All of life seems a bane
Caught in situations, festered in vain

And you God
In perfect stance
Direct indirectly
Neither being disturbed, nor disturbing

At life's end, when mortals rush
Your Grace fills, to wash our tears
From a broken heart, is a call for change
A stride too long, only fitting your clock.

Unburden my ship

I thought I could
Heavier grew the baggage
Till I couldn't bear further

I loosened to be lighter
For life is about a thousand surrenders
Before the final surrender.

Break my Pride

I winked at death
And borrowed time
To live slipped dreams
And gulp no pride

Years slipped by
At blink of an eye
Things froze to fall
I crumbled in pall

Grace from your home
Filled recesses of my mind
To show love in all forms
For time refused to wait.

Call of Universe

When summers equal winters
And the tick of clock has gone unheard
When bespectacled eyes
Have contended with lingering memories
Unlearning seems tougher
But for the call of the Universe.

Smooth transit

My weary me
No time to cry
You my better half
Have left me dry

Work on my platter
No time to chatter
Weathering storms yonder
I sail not to flee

Bolted or blue
From strength to strength
On plateau I tread
What reason is there to cry ?

Hands abound
All in love
To help me sail asmooth.

Universal consciousness

You are forever anyway by my side
Walking amidst peril and chaos
I am to dole you through
In manners you choose

When I see my loved ones
In tumultuous state
Be me
That you take over

If it be that I am in you
Through my faculty and what not
You will be the best me

Can I be avaricious ?
Asking for many experiences of you ?
Perhaps every experience you are to manifest
Would be ad infinitum
Of the one single experience you manifested
In complete

Since words fall short to describe you
I'll stop here.

Roopa R

Live on

We travelled together as souls
Meeting each other at times
Flaws I had a many
You too had no less

In time we learnt
Tricks of life's trade
Life is what we make of it
Were you the faster to learn ?

All life I took
That too to unlearn
For in unlearning I found back life
And you were forever serene and wise

Heavenly Gods decided in time we last
Favoring passion and love
In balance we fought
In love was freedom and thus we grew

When in life we had it all
Life caught up with time
With no screeching halt
But time amore

Sweet goodbyes
Whispering came your call
With life complete you transcended
To your higher self in all.

Love of a life time

Where from did you come ?
Wading winds amidst storms
Many a love have you transcended
Just to visit me

Time just is not enough
And one day is all we have
Thence we need to live life
As if life doled all of life

Mundane things we've got to deal
Breaching love, not parting ways
In time we meet
More than a fleet

No time is long
For your heavenly hands
No smile is just enough
For your thoughts which flow by

No words to speak
I close my eyes and reminisce
The moments of truth
Moments of love in complete.

Jealous

In seething rivalry I competed
All for nothing
Losing time, peace and all
Drawing negative energy from far and wide
With me in the centre of tide

Little did I realize
You are God's child
Uniqueness is nature
With every being

A hundred things to lay hands on
And many more to love
Why this measly me
Grounded never more ?

If I think not you my brethren
Would acceptance come galore ?
Wisdom on paper and peril in me
When will I ever grow ?

I looked for flaws within myself
Learning a secret, I forgave myself
Before asking for forgiveness.

Making of You

Think of it again
People are gone
And I won't be here long

When your teeth are broken
All one by one
Who is to lead you kindly
If with closed eyes we depart ?

It's no magic on earth
Or wishes of a time
That stand to work their way
It's your work of a lifetime

In paths you create
With muddy hands and unfurled mind
To make a man of you
In thy own eyes

Don't be cowed down
Or back away in fear
If I harp or scream
I'm unleashing time
For now I am I.

Roopa R

Thoughts ...up in smoke

I imagine
Holding
A lit cigar, ashes intact
Ashes to fall
Enblock
With one time useful
Feelings and thoughts
Now thoughts go in smoke
With no signs of cigar.

Life completed

Years ago
When in thoughts I was in penury
You walked by me
Hand in hand, distances long

My turn came too
Not so too soon
In wait for long

Distances we've travelled
In each other's mind
Listening now and then

By far the biggest listening
Came gushing through
When all dams broke down
And time stood still for me and you

God of death Yama
Morphed into God of time
Melting His stoned heart
Brimming love filled time

Little had I realized
What living in the moment meant
Till such time
All these were theory

With time as Grace
Every moment infinite
In the finality of things
Nothing left undone.

Genesis

When a dozen children were too many
And bringing them down was less than a penny
Yet the cry in the womb
Silenced minds
The pleading went aloud
A child was born.

(The above is in relation to feticide)

God's Grace

In my one life
I see both slowness as well fast
Is it in the healing
Or God's timing

Warped mind in slowness
Obsessed over thoughts
Looked down by others
As weird man and more

Then there are others
Having come out it all
By themselves or by others
Sailing ahead of all

God in His wisdom
While placed a crown on man
Expects man to realize
He is not all

When is this time
While God waits awhile
That man opens doors
And God's Grace overflows ?

Is there a time
When all noises become melody
Or all melody becomes noise
Is the power in me to score one within the other ?

Is time in everything
Or everything within time ?

Frozen memories

As love fills my mind
I miss your listening thought
In rapturous touch you, God, put a stop
You spoke to time and spaced it out

That we meet in time
Stories to tell and stories to listen
Some time and space
That ousts from the hidden

Strange it seems
One sense at a time
Taking time sitting in thee
Blending all to ease ?

In me, you dwell
With your touch sublime
In flavored talks
We have frozen time.

Expanding love

I know God, with You
A tsunami is no different from heaven
You welcome all unto You
And all arise from You
I've heard it time and again

Is *pralaya too something like tsunami ?
That way, every yesterday is a tsunami
And today beginning of a new world
Ever expanding unto itself

Looking around
A strict voice here and a loving gesture there
All boils down to actions of love
It rests in me to accept them all
That I too in expansion emulate You

For in expanding I grow in love
In moments those I am You
Offering perhaps in any form
Is life dancing all around.

(*pralaya indicates end of world)

Little brother

Years ago
When my sky parted and earth shattered
My hornet ruffled
You nested me

It's my turn now
To foster you
From a distance or so
That you're more than grown

Little brother
Angry be not
Give me a chance
That you grow in my love

Corroded that I am
Bear with me
When in anger I pout or shout
It doesn't mean a thing
I more than love you

You have your drudgery to cope
Your stresses harp at you
I'll learn to smile
And be with you.

Reminisce now
Neither all yesterdays were so bad
Breather of good times
Board games and cricket weathers

Longer innings let's begin
I for you
And you for me
It's never too late for love.

Earth's heavenly clock

One time my moral ethics
Almost choked me
Because of ambiguity
In time your grace and my luck saved me
Here I am free now, both in time
And relatively in bindings
Waiting for my path to unfold

I may raise my eyebrows
Being cerebral now and then
But life's struggle has brought me wisdom
To replace me with Thee

Earthly life is a slow pace
Because of entanglements
Am I ready to borrow your heavenly clock
To replace the earthly time ?

Live on love

Love God
You blessed me
Feelings imprinted
As long as I wanted

Need I want more ?
Earthly time suffice not
Your one sense of love
For all you is infinite

Sunshine lit and all
The wind Gods made way
Time too made time
And then sprang love

Then there was work
And love dispersed
In love I was I
And God you were you.

Dad

When you were there
The tall me
Never saw you much face to face
Now with you gone
I tremble to think what lies ahead

Tell me dad
Will the enormity of life
Rob living out of my life ?
My dancing floor has caved in
Before I've stepped to dance

Everything seems a puzzle
In darkness will I see light ?
I've heard it
But will I ever learn
That in the present is everything ?

Life no past

I saw in your eye
The softness of your voice
A bated breath you held
Till turned I all careless to a care

Many nights you waited
And days many more
Bearing crosses too many
All sigh hidden in smile

I wail not
In your leaving you've left behind
Things for me to gather
Strength and valor

Move on I must
For life lived can be limitless
While mortal remains have timed clocks
All life is history continuum.

Crippling minds

Alarm bells flow my way
Seeing your friends as foe
Two to a dozen
All not in a row

In guises unknown
Planned or unplanned
I wonder why
The weather Gods favor their way

Crippling minds
Creating sleepless nights
I go to tether
From wilder clutches of nether

That you king of kings
Act not a beggar
All madness is not in world out
It's in me and you.